ALBERT AND THE N

JAMES HYWEL
By Appointment to
Children's Imagination

Albert Mouse
DARTMOUTH's
MOST FA-MOUSE
EXPLORER

Albert and the Mayor of Dartmouth

The Adventures of Albert Mouse
Book Eight

James Hywel

OINK
BOOKS

First published by Oink Books 2023
Copyright © 2023 by James Hywel

All rights reserved. No part of this publication may be reproduced, stored or transmitted in any form or by any means, electronic, mechanical, photocopying, recording, scanning, or otherwise without written permission from the publisher. It is illegal to copy this book, post it to a website, or distribute it by any other means without permission.

James Hywel asserts the moral right to be identified as the author of this work.

James Hywel has no responsibility for the persistence or accuracy of URLs for external or third-party Internet Websites referred to in this publication and does not guarantee that any content on such Websites is, or will remain, accurate or appropriate.

Designations used by companies to distinguish their products are often claimed as trademarks. All brand names and product names used in this book and on its cover are trade names, service marks, trademarks and registered trademarks of their respective owners. The publishers and the book are not associated with any product or vendor mentioned in this book. None of the companies referenced within the book has endorsed the book.

Although the publisher and the author have made every effort to ensure that the information in this book was correct at press time, the publisher and the author assume no responsibility for errors, including grammar and spelling mistakes. They will endeavour to rectify these in future editions.

The Dartmouth Town emblem is the copyright of the Dartmouth Town Council.

Written for

Morgan & Josie

and

Mr Spike

Albert Books

The mouse who wanted to see the world

Albert and the smuggler Mickey Mustard

Albert takes to the sky

Albert and the runaway train

Albert buys a boat

Albert learns to swim

Albert's Christmas Adventure

Albert and the Mayor of Dartmouth

Chapter 1

Even though Albert could hear the noise of people going about their business outside, he was in no rush to get up this morning. There was clearly something troubling him.

As he lay in his bed there came the familiar tap on his bedroom window.

"It's open," said the little mouse in a loud voice.

The window gently opened and Big Tony poked his head into the room.

"What's wrong, are you ill?" he asked, looking at Albert.

"No, I'm just having some quiet time to think," said Albert.

Big Tony stepped onto the windowsill, then hopped across onto Albert's bed and sat down.

"What ya' thinking about?" he asked.

"That's the problem," said Albert. "I don't know what I should be thinking about, but I know there's something that's bothering me."

"I get that sometimes, then I realise that it's just that I'm hungry, so I go and get myself a pasty and feel better," said the gull.

"I fear this is more than just feeling hungry," sighed the little mouse.

Albert's friend thought for a little while.

"What?" asked Albert.

"Nothing, it's just that mentioning the word pasty has made me feel hungry. I might just pop out for a snack, do you want me to bring you something?" asked Big Tony.

"Mmm, a pasty as well, please," said Albert, realising he hadn't eaten breakfast yet.

"Right you are. I'll be back in two ticks."

With that, the gull hopped across to the windowsill and disappeared out of the window.

Once again Albert was alone in his room with his thoughts.

Chapter 2

As the little mouse lay in his bed trying to think about what was bothering him, there was a knock at the door.

"Yes, who is it?" he asked.

"Me," said his mother as she opened the door.

"Oh, morning Mum!"

"Albert Mouse, are you still in bed?" asked his mother looking surprised.

"Yes, but I've been awake a long time. I'm just lying here thinking, that's all," replied her son.

"Well, you can't think on an empty stomach so, come on, up you get and have some breakfast," said Mrs Mouse.

"It's ok, Big Tony's just gone to fetch me a pasty," said Albert.

"A pasty! Albert, that's not breakfast and, anyway, you don't know where it's been if Big Tony's fetching it."

"It's fine, Mum. Not everything Big Tony eats is from a bin, you know," said Albert.

"No, the rest is pinched from some poor unsuspecting tourist. Anyway, what are you thinking about?" asked his mother sitting down on the edge of Albert's bed.

"I'm not sure. I just feel troubled about something and I'm not sure what it is," said the little mouse.

"Well, you've been very busy lately and maybe you've overdone it," suggested his mother.

"No, it's not that. Well, I don't think it is."

"Is it your sisters? Because I know they annoy you quite a bit," said Mrs Mouse.

"They are quite annoying, but no, it's not that either."

"Well, whatever it is, it will all sort itself out. And remember, if you ever need to talk about anything you know you can talk to me," said his mother.

"Thanks, Mum," said Albert. "But I can also talk to Big Tony as well."

"Yes, well. I'm not always sure how much advice I'd want to take from him," sighed Mrs Mouse.

"Big Tony has some very good advice sometimes," said Albert, sticking up for his friend.

Just then there was a flutter of wings and Big Tony appeared at the window.

"Oh, hello, Mrs Mouse. How are you today?" asked the gull.

"I'm very well, thank you. We were just talking about you," said Mrs Mouse.

"All good I hope? Anyway, here's your pasty, Albert," said Big Tony handing a paper bag to the little mouse. "Eat up while it's still hot."

The gull noticed that Mrs Mouse was looking at the bag with suspicion.

"Don't worry, I didn't steal it. I bought it from the pasty shop in town. It cost me a whole pound!" said Big Tony.

Albert smiled at his Mum. He then broke his pasty in two and offered half to Big Tony.

"No thanks, I've already eaten mine on the way over here," said the gull.

"Right, well, I'll leave you to your breakfast. Try not to get crumbs all over the bed," said Albert's mother as she left the room.

Chapter 3

Albert tucked into his pasty while Big Tony made himself comfortable on the end of the bed.

"So, did you find out what was on your mind?" he asked.

"No, not yet. Mum tried to help but it wasn't anything she suggested," said Albert, trying not to talk with his mouth full.

"Well, I'm always here if you want to talk," said Big Tony.

"Yes, I told Mum that."

"That's good. I'm sure she feels happier knowing that I'm here for you if you need any advice," said the gull.

"Oh, she is. She was saying that just before you came back," replied Albert taking another bite of his pasty.

The gull looked happy.

"Mmm, this pasty is really good," said Albert.

"I think I know what might be worrying you," said Big Tony eventually.

"You do?" asked Albert, sounding very surprised.

"Yes. It's just a suggestion but we've not had an adventure for a while and it might be that."

Albert stopped chewing and thought for a moment. This was something that the little mouse hadn't considered.

"You know what, Big Tony? I think you might be right. It could be that," said Albert.

"So, where are we going?" asked the gull.

Albert took another bite of his pasty and thought.

"I'm not sure yet, but I'm sure I'll think of something," he said with a smile.

Chapter 4

Soon Albert had finished his breakfast. Now that his problem had been solved he looked much happier.

"Mmm, that was delicious," he said as scrunched up the paper bag and tossed it into his wastepaper basket.

"Breakfast is after all the most important meal of the day," said Big Tony.

"Is it?" asked Albert.

"Yes, your mother is always saying that."

"Yes, she is, isn't she," replied Albert with a smile.

"Anyway, I'd better be off. Let me know when you've thought of an adventure," said the gull and he bounced across to the window and was gone.

Albert quickly got dressed and then went to the bathroom to wash his face and clean his teeth. He then slid down the bannister rail and after several somersaults, landed in the hallway.

"I've been thinking about what might be troubling you," said his mother as Albert came into the lounge.

"Oh, it's ok. Big Tony has sorted it all out," said Albert, sitting down on the sofa.

"He has?" asked Mrs Mouse.

"Yes. He said I'm probably feeling this way because I've not been on an adventure for a while," said the little mouse.

"An adventure?" said his mother, with a worried look on her face.

"Yes. I don't know why I didn't think of it myself after all it's quite obvious really," said Albert.

"What kind of adventure?" asked his mother, still looking concerned.

"We haven't decided yet, but in a minute I'll go upstairs and sit in my window. From there, looking out over

Dartmouth, I'm sure something will come to me," said the little mouse.

"Well, you're not doing anything dangerous, that much I do know," said his mother.

"Mum, stop worrying. Not all my adventures are dangerous," said Albert.

"Oh really? So floating out to sea with the balloons wasn't dangerous? Then there was saving the steam train from crashing," said his mother.

"Mum, I'm still here, aren't I?" said her son.

"Yes, but that is more by good luck than good management. You are the only son I have and I don't want anything to happen to you that's all," said Mrs Mouse.

"Nothing's going to happen, Mum, I promise."

"Just promise you'll tell me what the adventure is before you do disappear off to ……,"

His mother paused and decided not to mention any faraway places in case it gave her son any ideas.

"Well, somewhere dangerous," she said finally.

"I promise," said Albert, getting off the sofa and going out into the garden.

Chapter 5

Albert jumped down the steps, then across the lawn and sat down on the bench. He soon felt the sun warming his fur and it made him feel happy.

"What are you smiling about?" asked Dorothy, who had also come outside and was now sitting on the steps.

"Just enjoying the sunshine," said Albert who didn't feel much like having a conversation with his sister.

"I heard you talking to Mum about going on an adventure," said Dorothy. "Where are you going?"

"I haven't decided yet," said Albert.

"Well, wherever it is, it will probably be boring!" said Dorothy.

"It will be very exciting if you must know. All my adventures are," said Albert, closing his eyes.

"Yes, exciting when you have to be rescued again," laughed his sister.

"I only needed rescuing once, and, anyway, that was before I became experienced," said Albert, who still had his eyes shut.

"Hmm, experienced in looking silly," said Dorothy.

"I do hope you're not trying to annoy your brother!" said Mrs Mouse who had suddenly appeared behind Dorothy.

"No," replied her daughter.

"Albert, there's a phone call for you," said Mrs Mouse.

"For me? Who is it?" asked Albert, quickly opening his eyes.

"They didn't say, only that they needed to talk to you quite urgently," said his mother.

"It's probably someone to let you know you've won the most irritating brother competition," laughed Dorothy.

"I said that's enough," said Mrs Mouse sternly.

Albert jumped off the bench and ran into the house.

Chapter 6

The little mouse rushed into the lounge and picked up the phone.

"Hello, Albert Mouse speaking."

"Hello Albert, this is David Wells, the Mayor of Dartmouth," said the voice.

"Hello, Sir," said Albert.

"I'm sorry to trouble you and I hope I wasn't disturbing you?"

"Not at all. I was just sitting in the garden and being annoyed by my sister," said Albert.

"The thing is, I was wondering if you had a moment to come and see me. I have something I need to talk to you about."

"I can come to your office now if you'd like?" said the little mouse.

"Great, the only thing is I'm not in my office," said the Mayor. "I'm in Torbay Hospital."

"Hospital?" gasped Albert. "Are you ok?"

"I'm fine. I'll explain everything when I see you," said the Mayor. "I'll send a car to pick you up and bring you here. Shall we say ten minutes?"

Albert looked at the clock on the mantlepiece.

"I'll be ready," said the little mouse.

"Great. The driver's name is Geoff, see you soon," said Mr Wells.

Albert put the phone down and then rushed upstairs to his bedroom.

"Gosh, the Mayor of Dartmouth wants to see me," he said to himself as he took his best white shirt out of the cupboard. "It must be important."

He then quickly put on his red bow tie and took his new cap off the shelf. After he had looked at himself in the mirror to make sure he looked smart enough to meet the Mayor of Dartmouth, the little mouse ran back downstairs.

"Mum, I have to go out urgently," he said.

"Hang on, who was on the phone?" asked his mother.

"The Mayor of Dartmouth and he needs to see me right away," said Albert.

"The Mayor? What does he want?"

"No idea, but he said he'd explain everything when I see him. He's sending a car to collect me," said the little mouse.

Just then Albert heard a car pull up outside.

"That's the car now," said Albert and ran out of the house.

"Wait, where are you going?" asked his mother.

"I'm going to the hospital," called Albert.

"The hospital?" called Mrs Mouse, but it was too late. Albert had already crawled under the gate.

Chapter 7

When the driver saw Albert, he got out of the car.

"Good morning, Albert Mouse," he said. "My name is Geoff, the Mayor has sent me to collect you."

"Morning, Geoff," said the little mouse as he got into the back of the car.

The car then sped away down Higher Street before turning left into Newcomen Road.

"How far is Torbay?" asked Albert, as the car passed the Royal Castle Hotel and onto the Mayor's Avenue.

"It's about twenty-two miles," said the driver. "Just sit back and relax. We should be there in less than an hour."

Back at No.10 Higher Street, Mrs Mouse was all of a fluster.

"I wonder what the Mayor wants with Albert?" she said, as she prepared lunch.

"Maybe Mickey Mustard has escaped and the Mayor needs Albert's help to track him down again," said Millie.

"No dear. If it was about Mickey Mustard the police would have called, not the Mayor" said her mother.

"True, I didn't think of that," said Millie. "What time will Albert be back?"

"I don't know, but I'm sure he will be back just as soon as he's finished."

Dorothy was still sitting on the step as Big Tony floated down from the roof and landed beside her.

"Have you seen Albert? I can't find him anywhere," he said.

"He's gone to the hospital," replied Dorothy, very matter-of-factly.

"Hospital! Why?" asked the gull.

"Probably to get a new brain," she said sarcastically.

"Oh no! Why didn't someone tell me?" and with that, he jumped into the air and flew as fast as he could to Dartmouth Hospital.

Just then Mrs Mouse came to the door.

"Dorothy, who were you talking to?" she asked.

"Just Big Tony. He wanted to know where Albert was, so I told him," answered Dorothy.

Mrs Mouse then went back inside the house.

Chapter 8

It took Big Tony less than a minute to reach Dartmouth Hospital on South Embankment.

"Hmm, that's a bit odd," he said, looking at the deserted building with its windows boarded up. "Looks like it's been closed."

Big Tony tried to think of any other hospitals in Dartmouth but couldn't think of any.

"Come on, think! Think! Where can they have taken Albert?" he said to himself.

Just then he had an idea.

"Of course, Mrs Gunn. She'll know if there is another hospital near here," he said and flew off to the Dartmouth Visitor Centre.

"Oh hello, Big Tony. Nice to see you. Where's Albert?" she asked when she saw the large gull arrive in the Centre.

"Albert's been taken to hospital," said Big Tony.

"Oh no! Is he alright? What's happened? Was he involved in an accident?" said Mrs Gunn, looking very distressed.

"To be honest, I have no idea what's happened to him, but his sister Dorothy said he had hurt his head. All I know is that he's been taken to hospital," said Big Tony.

"How did he hurt his head?" asked Mrs Gunn.

"No idea. Maybe he fell out of his bedroom window," said the gull.

"Oh, how awful!" said Mrs Gunn.

"The thing is I went to the hospital on South Embankment but it looks closed."

"Oh, that's been closed for a long time. The nearest hospitals are now in either Brixham, Totnes or Torbay," said Mrs Gunn.

"Ok, can you show them to me on a map?" asked the gull.

Mrs Gunn took Big Tony over to a large map on the wall and pointed to the three hospitals.

"Right, I'd start with the nearest first so that's Brixham, then Totnes and, finally, Torbay," said Big Tony as he tried to memorise the places in his head.

"Good idea," said Mrs Gunn opening the door to let Big Tony out. "Oh, I do hope Albert's ok."

"Let's hope so," said Big Tony as he flew into the air and headed towards Brixham.

Mrs Gunn then came back into the Visitor Centre and sat down in her office.

"Is everything ok?" asked one of the other ladies who worked at the centre.

"Albert Mouse has been involved in an accident and is in hospital," said Mrs Gunn.

"Oh no, that's awful! Is he going to be ok?"

"I don't know. It seems he fell out of his bedroom window, so it could be very serious," said Mrs Gunn.

Chapter 9

In the back seat of the Mayor's car, Albert was blissfully unaware of the confusion happening back in Dartmouth. He was too busy reading the signposts of the villages they were driving through; names like Halwell and Harbertonford were places Albert had never heard of.

Soon they arrived at a place called Totnes which was almost as big as Dartmouth. Then they drove through another place called Marldon.

"Just ten more minutes, Albert," said Geoff.

Back at No. 10 Higher Street, a white envelope dropped through the letterbox and then a blue one, then two yellow ones.

Mrs Mouse got up from her chair and went into the hallway.

Just then another envelope landed on the doormat.

She picked several of the envelopes up.

"Who are they for?" asked Millie.

"They all appear to be for Albert, but it's not his birthday," said her mother as another envelope dropped through the letterbox.

"Can we open them?" asked Millie.

"No, you should never open someone else's letters. It's very rude," said Mrs Mouse, placing the coloured envelopes on the sideboard.

As Mrs Mouse made her way back into the lounge, twelve more envelopes dropped onto the door mat.

"I'll get them!" shouted Millie.

"What's going on?" asked Dorothy, as she came downstairs with one of her dolls.

"Albert has received lots of letters. Look," said Millie holding up several of the envelopes. "And there are more on the cupboard."

Dorothy glanced at the large pile of envelopes.

"Mum, what's going on? Why is Albert getting all this mail?" she asked her mother.

"I'm not sure, but you know Albert. He is Dartmouth's most fa-mouse explorer after all. So, who knows? Maybe they are from his fans," sighed Mrs Mouse.

Just then the letterbox rattled again as several more envelopes landed on the doormat.

Chapter 10

Over in Torbay, the car turned into West Cadewell Way and pulled up outside the hospital.

"Here we are," said Geoff, as he opened the car door to let Albert out. "Follow me."

Albert had never been in a hospital before and it all looked very strange.

Geoff went up to the reception desk and spoke to a lady in a blue uniform.

"I'm sorry, but visiting times are over, you'll have to come back at three o'clock," she said.

"But we are here to see David Wells, the Mayor of Dartmouth. It's very important town business and he is expecting us," said Geoff.

"Us?" asked the lady looking around for a second person.

Geoff bent down and picked Albert up and placed him on the counter.

"Oh, Albert Mouse! I'm a big fan of yours," said the lady.

"Hello," said Albert, shaking her hand. "I'm very pleased to meet you but we really need to see the Mayor urgently."

"Of course. I'll just get you the room number."

"It's ok, we know where the Mayor is," said Geoff, lifting Albert down off the counter.

They went through doors, along corridors and then through more doors until Albert had no idea where he was.

Eventually, Geoff stopped at a door and knocked, before opening it.

"Albert! It's so good to see you," said Mr Wells, who was lying in a bed.

"I got here as quickly as I could," said Albert, shaking the Mayor's hand. "Are you ill?"

"Not ill exactly, but I broke my leg coaching the Torquay Colts rugby team," said the Mayor tapping the white cast that was on his leg.

"Is it sore?" asked Albert.

"No, it's fine. It looks far worse than it is," said Mr Wells.

"So, you said you wanted to see me, Sir," said Albert, climbing onto a chair beside the bed.

"Please, call me David," said the Mayor. "Oh, would you like a cup of tea and some biscuits?"

"Mmm, yes please," said Albert, even though he'd just eaten a pasty.

Geoff nodded and disappeared to get some tea and biscuits, leaving the Mayor and Albert alone.

Chapter 11

In Dartmouth, more and more envelopes arrived at Albert's house. There were so many that very soon they were heaped up all over the lounge and covered most of the kitchen.

"I really think we should open at least one envelope to see what it says," suggested Millie.

"No, I've already told you, they have Albert's name on them so they are private," said Mrs Mouse, moving several envelopes off the sofa so she could sit down.

Just then there was a knock at the door.

"I'll get it!" said Dorothy, running to the door.

"A delivery for Albert Mouse," said the courier driver standing at the door holding three large baskets of flowers. "Sign here, please."

"Mum, you'd better help me," called Dorothy, as she signed her name.

"Goodness!" said Mrs Mouse as she came into the hallway. "Are they for Albert as well?"

Dorothy looked at the small card that was attached to one of the baskets.

"Yes, they are all for him," said Dorothy.

Before Mrs Mouse could say anything, there was another knock at the front door.

"That had better be Albert," said Mrs Mouse, as she opened the door.

"Delivery for Albert Mouse," said a man holding a large basket of fruit.

Mrs Mouse placed the basket on the floor next to the flowers and closed the door.

Meanwhile Big Tony had been to Brixham Hospital but Albert wasn't there, so the gull had flown to Totnes

Hospital, but the news was the same. No sign of Albert.

Big Tony was now becoming very worried about his best friend and raced as fast as he could to Torbay Hospital.

Chapter 12

The Mayor of Dartmouth looked a little uncomfortable as if he was trying to find the right words.

"What is it?" asked the little mouse.

"Albert, I need to ask you a massive favour," said Mr Wells.

"No problem, David. You know I'm always happy to help the town if I can," replied the little mouse.

"The thing is, the doctors have told me I have to rest for a few days," said Mr Wells, sounding rather embarrassed.

"And you want me to coach the Torquay Colts?" said Albert excitedly.

"No, something more important than that, Albert. I need you to be Mayor for a few days."

"The Mayor!?" gasped Albert.

"I know it's a big ask, but you're the only person I could think of and it will only be for a day or two."

"Yes, please!" said Albert, jumping for joy.

"Really?" asked the Mayor. "Oh Albert, I knew I could count on you."

"When do I start?" asked Albert.

"Well, right away, I suppose. But first I need you to swear an oath to Dartmouth," said the Mayor.

"Oh, I don't think I can do that. My Mum says only vagabonds and no-gooders swear," said Albert, looking disappointed.

The Mayor laughed.

"No, Albert, it's not that kind of swear. It's like a promise, only a very big promise. It's called the Declaration of Acceptance of Office."

"Oh, I can do that. I'm good with promises," smiled Albert.

"Ok, hold your right hand up like this and repeat after me....,"

Albert held up his right hand.

"I, Albert Mouse, having been elected to the office of member of Dartmouth

Town Council declare that I take that office upon myself, and will duly and faithfully fulfil the duties of it according to the best of my judgement and ability. I undertake to observe the code as to the conduct which is expected of members of Dartmouth Town Council," said Mr Wells.

Albert repeated the declaration.

"Congratulations! You are now the Mayor of Dartmouth," said Mr Wells shaking Albert's hand.

"Wow, really? That was easy," said Albert.

"Yes, that's the easy part," said Mr Wells as Geoff returned with a tray of tea and biscuits.

Chapter 13

Big Tony glanced down from high above Torbay and searched for the hospital.

"That must be it," he said to himself as he noticed a few ambulances parked outside a large building.

The gull circled several times and then came to land in front of the main entrance.

"Hello, can I help you?" asked the lady at reception as Big Tony walked in.

"Yes, I hope so. I'm looking for Albert Mouse, a small chap about so high with a long tail. He's my best friend," said the gull.

"Yes, he's in room 126, through those doors," said the lady.

"Thank you," said Big Tony and he waddled off as fast as he could towards the doors.

As he went, he looked at all the room numbers and eventually reached a door that said Room 126, and knocked.

"Come in," said a man's voice.

"Odd," thought Big Tony, who was expected to hear Albert's voice. "Maybe it's the doctor."

The gull pushed the door open.

"Big Tony! What are you doing here?" asked Albert putting his cup of tea down.

"Albert, what are you doing? Shouldn't you be resting?" asked the gull looking concerned.

The gull then looked at the man lying in Albert's bed.

"Who are you and why are you in Albert's bed? Shame on you, don't you know he's just had a brain transplant and needs to be resting!" said Big Tony, sounding very angry.

"Erm, excuse me?" asked Mr Wells.

"You heard me, a brain transplant. Now, I'm not an expert but I do know that it's quite a serious procedure, so come on, up you get and let Albert get back into bed," said the gull.

Mr Wells looked at Albert who was just as confused as he was.

"Big Tony, I've not had a brain transplant, look," said Albert showing Big Tony the top of his head.

"Sorry, but Dorothy said you'd been taken to the hospital."

"Yes, but only to see Mr Wells," said Albert, pointing to the man in the bed. "He has broken his leg and needs my help."

"I asked to see Albert because I need him to be Mayor of Dartmouth for a few days," said Mr Wells.

"But we already have a Mayor in Dartmouth," said Big Tony.

"Yes, me. I'm the Mayor," said Mr Wells.

"So, you're not going to die?" asked Big Tony, looking at Albert.

Albert shook his head.

"Oh, I'm so confused," said Big Tony, picking up a biscuit.

"Albert, why don't you explain everything to Big Tony on the way back to Dartmouth?" said Mr Wells.

"Good idea," agreed the little mouse finishing his cup of tea.

"Geoff will take you home, then tomorrow you can go straight to my office at the Town Hall. On my desk, you will find my diary and in it are all my appointments for the next two days. If there are any problems just call me," said Mr Wells.

"Understood," said Albert.

"Oh, I almost forgot," said Mr Wells, opening his bedside cupboard and taking out a large gold chain.

He then removed a small gold badge from it and handed it to Albert.

"This is the badge of office and you'll need to wear it at all times."

Albert pinned the badge on his shirt and then said goodbye to Mr Wells.

Chapter 14

Albert and Big Tony then followed Geoff back along the corridor and past the reception desk.

"Oh, sorry to bother you both, but do you think I could have a photo with you and Big Tony?' asked the lady at the desk.

"Of course!" said Albert.

Once Albert had signed a few autographs, they got into the car and headed back to Dartmouth.

"Right, so explain to me what's going on?" asked Big Tony.

"The Mayor rang me and said he wanted to see me. Geoff picked me up and drove me to the hospital, where David was resting after breaking his leg," said Albert.

"Who is David?" asked Big Tony.

"Mr Wells," sighed the little mouse.

"Right, so David is also Mr Wells, who is also the Mayor?" asked the gull.

"Yes. He said the doctors had told him to rest for two days and he asked if I would be Mayor while he got better. Of course, I agreed. Then you arrived," said Albert.

"So, now you're the Mayor of Dartmouth?" asked Big Tony.

"Yes, but only for two days, then Mr Wells will be the Mayor again," said Albert.

"Right, I'm still a bit confused why Dorothy said you were having a new brain but I guess we will find out when we get home," said Big Tony.

Chapter 15

As the car turned off Smith Street and into Higher Street, Albert was a little surprised.

"Who are all these people?" he asked, looking at the large crowd that had gathered outside his house.

"I'm afraid I can't get through, so I'll have to drop you here," said Geoff as he pulled up outside The Shambles.

Albert and Big Tony said goodbye and got out of the car.

"Do you think something has happened?" asked Albert.

"Albert, it might be best if you wait here while I go and find out," said Big Tony.

Albert began to get a sick feeling in his stomach and hoped his family were ok.

"What's happened?" Big Tony asked a small girl who was standing outside the River & Rose.

"We're waiting for news about Albert," said the little girl.

"Yes, he's had an accident and been taken to hospital in a helicopter," said the girl's mother.

Big Tony crept quietly back to Albert.

"What is it?" asked Albert. "Is it bad news?"

"Erm, I'm not sure. The thing is, everyone thinks you've had an accident and been taken to hospital in a helicopter.

"What? Well, who told them that?" asked Albert.

"Not sure, but we'll sort that out later. First, we need to get you into the house without these people seeing you. Then we can find out what's happened and how all this started," said Big Tony.

"Do you have a plan?" asked the little mouse.

"Not really," said Big Tony.

Just then a delivery van pulled up and a man climbed out of the van.

"Excuse me please, I need to make a delivery to No.10," said the driver as he walked towards the crowd holding a basket of fruit.

"I do!" said Albert to Big Tony, as he ran across the street and jumped into the basket.

While the delivery man fought his way through the crowds, the little mouse quickly hid under an apple and two bananas.

Eventually, the delivery man managed to open the gate and then knocked at the front door of No.10.

"Not another delivery," said Mrs Mouse opening the door and taking the basket. "Thank you."

Mrs Mouse then put the basket on the floor with all the others and closed the door.

"I'll be glad when Albert gets himself back here," she said. "And what are all these people doing outside the house?"

Albert crawled out from under the apple and looked at the assorted baskets and piles of envelopes.

"Mum, what's going on?" said the little mouse, as he climbed out of the basket.

Chapter 16

"Albert, what are you doing in the basket?" asked his mother.

"I needed to get past all those people standing outside," said Albert. "What is going on and where has all this stuff come from?"

"I thought you could tell me," said his mother, looking cross.

Albert picked up one of the envelopes and opened it.

"That's odd," said Albert, reading the card and then passing it to his mother.

"Get well soon?" said Mrs Mouse. "Why are you receiving get-well cards?"

"I'm not sure, but I think we need to talk to Dorothy," said Albert.

"Don't you try and blame your sister, young man. I know this has something to do with you," said his mother.

Just then Big Tony came down the stairs.

"Sorry, I had to come in through the upstairs window. I'm afraid Albert is right. I think we need to talk to Dorothy," said the gull.

"Dorothy Mouse, get yourself down here this instant," called Mrs Mouse.

Albert's sister slowly came down into the lounge where her mother was sitting with Albert and Big Tony.

"When Big Tony spoke to you this morning and asked where I was, what did you say?" asked Albert.

"Hospital," replied Dorothy, shrugging her shoulders.

"Then when I asked why was Albert in hospital what did you say?" asked Big Tony.

Dorothy muttered something under her breath.

"Speak up, Dorothy," said her mother.

"I said that Albert was probably going to the hospital to get a new brain," said her daughter.

"I assumed that Dorothy was telling the truth, so in a panic, I went to the Dartmouth Visitor Centre and told Mrs Gunn that Albert had gone to the hospital. She and the staff were as worried as I was. I then flew to Brixham Hospital, then Totnes Hospital and eventually found Albert at the hospital in Torbay," said Big Tony.

"I'm sorry," said Dorothy.

"Mum knew I was meeting the Mayor of Dartmouth and that he was in the hospital," said Albert.

"I'm sorry," said Dorothy, again.

"It seems you have made a lot of people worry for nothing. Just look at all those people out there and at all these get well cards and flowers," said Big Tony.

"I'm sorry," said Dorothy, again.

"I should think you are, young lady. I hope you've learned a valuable lesson that one silly joke can be misunderstood and spread. And that before you know it, it's caused all sorts of problems," said her mother.

"What are we going to do now?" asked Dorothy looking upset.

"The first thing I need to do is tell everyone outside that I'm home and well," said Albert getting out of the chair.

"No, Albert. I'll do it," said his mother.

Mrs Mouse got up and opened the front door to speak to the crowd of well-wishers.

"Hello, everyone. I have some news about Albert. I'm pleased to say he is well and resting upstairs. He would like me to thank you for all your get-well cards and flowers," she said.

"Three cheers for Albert! Hip hip hooray, hooray, hooray!" shouted the crowd.

Slowly one by one the people went home and High Street returned to normal.

Chapter 17

Mrs Mouse went into the kitchen and put the kettle on.

"Albert, what was it that the Mayor wanted to see you about, anyway?" she asked.

"Oh, yes, I almost forgot. He's made me Mayor of Dartmouth for a few days while he rests his broken leg," said Albert, as he and Big Tony opened some more of the cards.

"No, really, what did he want?" asked his mother, as she placed a large cake on the coffee table.

"It's true, Mrs Mouse," said Big Tony. "Albert, show your Mum the badge."

The little mouse pointed to Mayor's badge that was still pinned on his shirt.

"So, what do you have to do as Mayor?" asked his mother.

"I'm not really sure yet," said Albert. "But first thing tomorrow morning I have to go to my office at the Town Hall and read the diary. Mr Wells says it's all written in there."

Albert then looked around at all the baskets of flowers and fruit.

"Maybe as Mayor, I could send some of these flowers to the hospitals to cheer the places up?" said Albert

"They do look like they need cheering up," said Big Tony.

"Mum, I'm sure we can't eat all this fruit so, maybe, we can just take some apples for an apple pie, and then the rest we could donate to the food bank for people who don't have much food," said the little mouse.

"I think that would be a lovely idea, Albert," said Mrs Mouse.

"See, Mum, I already have things to do as Mayor of Dartmouth."

Just then there was a knock at the door.

"I'll get it," said Albert and he opened the front. "Oh, hello, Mrs Saunders."

"Albert, I heard you fell out of your bedroom window, are you alright?" she asked.

"I'm fine. It was a bit of a misunderstanding, that's all," said the little mouse.

"Thank goodness for that. I've had enough stress for one day what with moving the shop," she said.

"The what?" said Albert, looking shocked.

"Oh, didn't you hear? We are moving to 9A Foss Street," said Mrs Saunders. "It's not too far away so you'll still be able to visit and borrow books."

Mrs Saunders then said goodbye and hurried back to the bookshop.

"Who was that?" asked Mrs Mouse.

"It was Mrs Saunders. Did you know the bookshop is moving to Foss Street?" asked Albert, as he came back into the lounge.

"No, but it's only a few streets away so you'll still be able to pop down and see her," said Albert's mother.

"Hmm, it's just that everything seems to be changing," sighed Albert.

That evening before he went to sleep, Albert arranged his best clothes ready for his big day at the Mayor's office. His mother had ironed him a clean white shirt and pressed his trousers. He then placed the Mayor's badge under his pillow where he knew it would be safe.

The little mouse looked out of his window at the bookshop and sighed again.

Albert then climbed into bed, closed his eyes and went to sleep.

Chapter 18

Albert woke up very early the next morning and went to the bathroom to wash his face and clean his teeth. After he had dressed the little mouse went downstairs.

"You're up bright and early this morning," said his mother as Albert came into the kitchen.

"Yes, I don't want to be late for my first day as Mayor," he said, pouring some cereals into a bowl.

"You certainly don't. Oh, I've taken a few apples out to make a pie and the rest of the fruit is by the front door," said Mrs Mouse.

"Good, I'll get Big Tony to collect it all this morning," said Albert as he ate his breakfast.

"Big Tony will never be able to carry all that stuff," said his mother.

"I'm sure the Town Council has a van," said Albert. "If not, I'll see if Geoff is busy."

"Who's Geoff?"

"The man who drove me to Torbay to meet the Mayor," said Albert.

The little mouse looked at the clock on the kitchen wall.

"Well, I'd better go to the office then," he said getting down from the table.

"Ok, have you got everything?" asked his mother.

The little mouse checked he had put on his bow tie, which he had.

"My badge!" he said in a panic and ran upstairs.

Moments later he came back into the kitchen.

"Phew, that was lucky," said patting the badge which was now pinned on his shirt.

"Well, you have a wonderful day. I'm so proud of you, your first day at work," said his mother hugging him.

"Thanks, Mum."

"And make sure you have lunch because I know what you're like."

"I will, see you later, Mum."

Albert walked down through the garden and opened the gate.

"Morning, Mr Mayor," said Geoff, who was standing next to the car.

"Morning, Geoff. What are you doing here?"

"Taking you to work. You didn't think we'd let you walk up to Victoria Road, did you?"

Albert then realised he didn't know where the Mayor's office was.

"Thanks," he said as he climbed into the back seat.

Suddenly the little mouse realised that he had forgotten something else.

"Wait!" he said, rolling down the window. "We need to wait for Big Tony!

Albert rolled the window and called to his friend.

The large gull swooped down from a rooftop and jumped in through the window.

"Sorry I'm late, I was just finishing my breakfast," said Big Tony.

"Ready?" asked Geoff.

Albert held his thumb up and the car slowly drove off.

Chapter 19

It only took a few minutes for the car to arrive at the large stone building on Victoria Street.

"Wow, it has a flag!" said Albert excitedly. "Is that all my office?"

"No, there are a lot of people who work in the building. You just have one of the rooms," said Geoff, as he turned off the car engine.

Geoff then led Albert and Big Tony up the metal steps that went up to the first floor of the building.

"Good morning, Mayor," said a lady at the front desk. "My name is Melanie,

I'm so pleased to meet you. I'm one of your biggest fans. Let me introduce you to everyone."

Albert was then introduced to all the other people who worked in the council offices. Soon he was quite tired from shaking everyone's hand.

"And this is your office, said Melanie.

"Wow, it's bigger than my bedroom!" said the little mouse as he looked around.

"I'll just go and make you both a drink," said Melanie, as she left Albert to make himself at home.

"Wow, look at this place," said Big Tony, settling himself down in a large chair.

Melanie soon returned with a tray with two cups and a plate of biscuits.

"I thought I'd make you a hot chocolate instead of coffee as I hear it's your favourite," she said placing the tray on the desk.

"Mmm, it is, thank you so much," said the little mouse.

"My pleasure. If you need anything just pick up the phone and I'll be happy to help," and Melanie went back to her desk.

As the two friends drank their hot chocolate, Albert remembered the flowers and fruit that were at his house. He picked up the phone.

"Hello Melanie, it's Albe ...., I mean the Mayor here. Do we have a van or a minibus that can go to my house and collect some baskets of fruit and take them to the food bank please?" asked Albert. "Yes, the one at Townstal Community Hall on Davis Road."

Albert then held his hand over the mouthpiece and spoke to Big Tony.

"Melanie says there is another one at Church Hill in Kingswear."

"Let's drop half the fruit there and half in Dartmouth," suggested Big Tony.

"Good idea!"

"Hello, yes, we will drop half the fruit in Dartmouth and half in Kingswear. Oh, there are also a lot of flowers, so can we drop those at Torbay Hospital to cheer the patients up?" said Albert and then put the phone down.

"All sorted. The minibus and a driver will be outside in ten minutes," said Albert, feeling pleased with himself.

Big Tony gathered up the remaining biscuits and went downstairs to help the van driver with the deliveries.

Albert then opened the large red diary that was on his desk.

Chapter 20

As he checked his appointments the telephone on his desk rang.

"Hello, the Mayor of Dartmouth. How may I help you?" said Albert.

"Morning, Albert, it's David. I'm just checking that you're settling in ok," said Mr Wells.

"Oh, good morning, David. Yes, everything is perfect. Melanie has just made me a cup of hot chocolate and everyone is being very kind and helpful. How are you feeling today?"

"I'm well and feeling much happier now that I know Dartmouth is in safe hands," said Mr Wells.

"It's a long story, but I have a lot of fruit at home and I've arranged for it to be delivered to the food banks in Dartmouth and Kingswear. Big Tony is supervising it all. I hope that's ok?" asked Albert.

"That's very kind of you Albert, thank you so much. Well, I'll not disturb you anymore, but if you have any problems just give me a call," said Mr Wells.

"I will and don't worry, Dartmouth is in safe hands. Goodbye," said Albert and he put the phone down.

"Right, so let's see what's next for me to do," said the little mouse looking again at the diary.

"Hmm, I don't have any appointments until eleven o'clock," he said as he glanced at the clock.

An idea suddenly came to him and he picked up the phone again.

"Hello Melanie, has Big Tony left in the minibus yet?" he asked.

"Erm, no, but they are just about to leave. Do you want me to stop them?"

"Yes, please, I'm coming right down."

Albert rushed out of his office.

"Hey, Albert, what's up?" asked Big Tony.

"I've just had an idea. Since you are going to Torbay Hospital after dropping off the fruit, is it possible to see if anyone needs a lift to the hospital? I mean, you're going there, anyway, and I'm sure there are a lot of elderly people who may find getting there difficult."

"Good idea, Albert. I'll sort it," said the gull.

Albert waved goodbye as the minibus drove off and then he went back into the building.

"Hello, did you catch Big Tony?" asked Melanie.

"Yes, thanks. I've just checked my diary and I have two hours before my first appointment of the day so I've decided I'm going to visit the people of Dartmouth and say hello," said the little mouse.

"What, on the streets?"

"No, in their house and I'm going start with everyone in Victoria Road," said Albert.

"Do you want someone to come with you?" asked Melanie, looking a little worried.

"No, I'll be fine," said the little mouse as he headed out of the door and into the street.

Chapter 21

Albert looked up and down the road and soon realised that there were quite a few houses, more than he had expected. The little mouse took his watch out of his pocket.

"Oh, well, I suppose if I start on one side of the road for one hour and then come back down the other I should be back in time for my first appointment."

Albert then knocked on the first door at No. 61.

"Hello, can I help you?" asked the lady who opened the door.

"I just wanted to introduce myself. My name is Albert Mouse and I'm the Mayor of Dartmouth," he said. "I just wanted to say hello."

"The Mayor?" asked the lady.

"That's right," said Albert pointing to his badge.

"Are you collecting money for something?"

Albert looked confused.

"No, I'm just visiting all the people who live in Dartmouth and saying hello to them," said the little mouse.

The lady started to look less cross.

"Well, that's really very kind of you. Would you like a cup of tea?" she asked.

"No, thank you. I've just had a hot chocolate and I've got a lot of houses to visit today. Anyway, it was lovely to meet you and if you need anything or have any problems that I should know about just let me know. My office is just next door," said Albert.

"I will. It's so nice to meet you, Albert," said the lady.

Albert then knocked at No. 63, then at No. 65.

Soon he had met lots of people and they all seemed very pleased that he had visited them.

After he had introduced himself to the very posh man who lived at No. 183 the little mouse looked at his watch.

"Gosh it's time to do the other side of the street now," he said to himself.

Albert was just about to cross the road when he noticed some people with bright yellow reflective waistcoats standing next to some bushes so he went over to see what they were doing.

"Hello, my name is Albert Mouse and I'm the Mayor of Dartmouth," he said.

"You look very busy this morning, what are you doing?"

"We are the Dartmouth Litteracy Society and we're picking up rubbish," said one lady, holding up a large black bag.

"Where from?" asked Albert looking around.

"From the sides of the roads and green areas like this," she said, pointing to the patch of grass. "People just throw away all sorts of rubbish. Look, here is a can someone has thrown away."

Albert looked shocked.

"Why don't they put it in the bin?" he asked.

"That's a good question," sighed the lady. "People just don't care anymore, Albert, that's the problem."

"Well, I'm pleased that you are around to make Dartmouth look clean and tidy. I hope you get paid a lot of money because you are doing a wonderful job," said Albert.

"Oh, we don't get paid," said the lady. "We are all volunteers."

"Wow, well on behalf of everyone in Dartmouth I'd like to thank you very much," said Albert shaking everyone's hand.

The little mouse then said goodbye and crossed the road. He first knocked at No. 124, then 121 until after another hour he was back outside the council offices.

Chapter 22

Before Albert went back into the building, he sat down on the metal steps and had a rest. He was quite exhausted from his long walk.

While he sat there, he thought about all the lovely people he had met. He had no idea that so many people lived in Dartmouth.

Albert then thought about the group of people he'd met that were giving their time for free to pick up other people's rubbish.

Just then there was a voice behind him.

"Ah, there you are Albert, is everything ok?"

Albert looked up and saw it was Melanie.

"Oh, I'm fine," said Albert. "Just a bit tired. I had no idea there were so many houses."

"How far did you get?"

"Right up to No. 183," said the little mouse.

"No wonder you're tired, that's a long way. I bet everyone appreciated your visit," said Melanie.

"Yes, they all seemed pleased to see me and they were all very nice and friendly. I also met some people gathering up rubbish from the street," said Albert.

"From the street?" asked Melanie, trying to think if it was bin day or not.

"Yes, they said they were from the Dartmouth Litteracy Society. Did you know that they do that for free? No one pays them," said the little mouse.

"Yes, there are some very nice people about, Albert."

"Yes, and some people who just throw rubbish on the roads and don't seem to love Dartmouth as much as I do," said Albert, sadly.

"It takes all sorts of people, Albert. We can only hope that there are more kind people than bad," said Melanie. "Anyway, would you like me to make you a nice hot chocolate before your appointment with Dartmouth Caring?"

"Mmm, that would be lovely, thank you!" said Albert getting up.

Chapter 23

After Albert had finished his hot chocolate it was time for him to go on his first official visit as the Mayor of Dartmouth. Geoff drove the little mouse to the Memory Cafe at Dartmouth Baptist Church on Carey Road.

Albert stepped out of the car and waved to the people who had gathered outside to see him.

"Hello Albert, welcome to the Memory Cafe, my name is Kay Pratley," said a very kind-looking lady. "Let me introduce you to our staff. This is Buffy, Natasha, Sarah, Ellie, Gill, Beryl and Tom."

Albert shook everyone's hand and was then taken into the Memory Cafe.

"So, tell me what it is you do here?" asked Albert trying to sound very grown up.

"Well, we are part of Dartmouth Caring and we provide an informal meeting place for people to come to with memory problems. We have a range of activities they can participate in, including crafts, games, and music, but the visitors can also talk to each other about their childhoods and when they were young," said Kay.

"That sounds really interesting," said Albert. "Can I meet some of the visitors today?"

"Of course, we have two ladies who are looking forward to meeting you," she replied, as she took Albert across the room to where the ladies were sitting.

"Albert, I'd like to introduce you to Angela Widdicombe."

"I'm very pleased to meet you," said Albert, shaking Angela's hand. "Have you lived in Dartmouth long?"

"Oh, I was born in Dartmouth and have lived here all my life," said Angela smiling.

"Wow, just like me then!" said Albert excitedly.

The little mouse then turned to the lady who was sitting next to Angela.

"Hello, and what is your name?" he asked very politely.

"My name is Judith Goatcher. Angela and I are cousins," she said shaking Albert's hand.

"I'm very pleased to meet you, Judith," he said. "I don't have any cousins, well, I don't think I do. I bet you have lots of stories about Dartmouth?"

"Oh, we do Albert. It's changed so much here since we were your age."

The little mouse listened as the two ladies told him of how Dartmouth used to be long before he was born. Albert was really surprised to hear that as children, many of them gave some of their pocket money to help build the outdoor swimming pool.

"That's where I learnt to swim," said Albert. "With a bit of help from my friend Daisy."

Albert said goodbye to Angela and Judith, and then met some of the other visitors. As he talked to the visitors. He soon realised that his childhood had been very easy compared to children many years ago.

Finally, his visit was over and the little mouse said goodbye to everyone.

"Please come and visit us again soon," said the volunteers and staff.

"I will, I promise," said the little mouse as he got back in the car.

As the car turned left into Townstal Road, Geoff looked in the rearview mirror.

"Do you want me to drop you anywhere for lunch?" he asked.

"Gosh, is it lunchtime already?" said Albert.

The little mouse then thought about the people who he'd seen gathering rubbish.

"Geoff, can you take me to the Wheelhouse in town, please?"

"Good choice," said Geoff.

A few minutes later, the car stopped outside the Wheelhouse Takeaway.

"Just wait here, I'll only be a minute," said Albert as he climbed out of the car. "Would you like anything, Geoff?"

"No thanks, Albert, I have a sandwich in my bag," said Geoff.

Albert quickly ran into the Wheelhouse.

Chapter 24

After a short time, he returned with three large carrier bags.

"You're not going to eat all that yourself, are you?" laughed Geoff.

Albert giggled.

"No, it's for some people I met this morning. I think they might be up near the end of Victoria Road somewhere by now. They should be easy to spot though," said the little mouse.

Albert was right. They found the group of volunteers in their bright yellow safety vests, still picking up rubbish.

"There they are! Can you drop me here," said Albert. "Oh, can you do me a favour, Geoff? I don't have any more appointments this afternoon, so please can you tell Melanie that after I've eaten my lunch here I'll be helping them to gather up some rubbish? Could you pick me up at about three o'clock?"

"Not a problem, Albert. I'll see you at three," said Geoff and drove back into town.

"Hello Albert, are you still doing house visits?" asked the lady he had spoken to earlier.

"No, I just thought I'd bring you some lunch," he said.

"Albert, that's really kind of you, but this must have cost a lot of money," said the lady. "My name is Andora, by the way."

"Hello, Andora. No, it didn't actually cost me anything. I told the nice man at the Wheelhouse that I was getting it for you, so I could say thank you for tidying Dartmouth up and he said there was no charge. There are some drinks in there as well," smiled Albert. "The very small packet of fish and chips is for me."

"Albert, let me introduce you to everyone," said Andora. "This is Sophie, Elaine, Isla, Finley, Sarah, Oli, Andy, Chris, Ruth, Hazel and Sam."

"I'm very pleased to meet you all," said Albert, shaking everyone's hand.

Albert then sat on the grass with his new friends and together they ate their lunch.

"Well, I have to say, Albert, that was delicious!" said Andora.

"I'm glad," smiled the little mouse. "Do you think I can help you pick up some rubbish? I don't have to be back at my office for a few hours yet."

"That's really kind of you Albert," said Andora and she gave him a black bin bag and a litter picker.

Soon the little mouse had filled three bags of rubbish. Just as he reached for a fourth bag, Geoff arrived with the car to pick him up again.

Albert said goodbye to everyone and climbed into the car.

"Hello Geoff, thanks for picking me up."

"You're very welcome, Albert. Did they enjoy their lunch?"

"They did, and then I helped them pick up some rubbish. You won't believe what people throw out of their car windows," said Albert.

"Oh, I would Albert, it's rather disgusting," said Geoff.

Back at the council offices Albert washed his hands and went to his office.

Chapter 25

"Ah, there you are, Albert," said Big Tony who was sitting in one of the chairs.

"Hi, Big Tony, how did you get on today?"

"Good. I dropped off the fruit at the food banks, then we took seven people to the hospital for their appointments. The flowers have really cheered the patients up. Oh, and I went to visit Mr Wells," said the gull. "He thanked us for all our hard work and said he'll call you tomorrow. How was your day?"

Albert sat down at his desk.

"To be honest, I'm exhausted. I walked up and down Victoria Road introducing myself to the residents. Then I went to The Memory Cafe and heard about what Dartmouth was like before I was even born which was amazing. Then I helped the Dartmouth Litteracy Society gather up rubbish."

"Phew, no wonder you're tired. What did you have for lunch?" asked Big Tony.

"My favourite," smiled Albert.

"Fish and Chips!" said the gull.

"Yes. You?"

"I had a burger in the hospital café, Mr Wells paid for it," said the gull.

Albert looked at his diary.

"Well, it looks like we are done for today, so, if you're ready, shall we go home and see if my Mum has got some cake?" asked Albert.

"Good idea."

Albert said goodnight to everyone at the council offices and then Geoff drove the two friends back to No.10 Higher Street.

"Mum, Albert's back!" shouted Millie as the car pulled up outside the gate.

Mrs Mouse rushed to the door to meet Albert and Big Tony.

"There is my wonderful boy, so, how was your day?" she said hugging him.

"Being Mayor is very tiring," said the little mouse.

"What about you Big Tony? Did the food bank like the fruit?" Mrs Mouse asked as she led them into the house.

"They did, and the hospital loved the flowers too."

"That's wonderful. Well, you both sit yourself down and I'll make you some hot chocolate," said Albert's mother.

"Do you have any cake?" asked Big Tony. "I've not eaten anything since lunch."

While Mrs Mouse prepared things in the kitchen, the two friends sat on the sofa and their eyes started to close.

By the time Mrs Mouse came in with the tray of cake, they were both fast asleep.

"Oh, bless them, they are both worn out," she said, placing a blanket over them and then closing the lounge door.

Chapter 26

As the time for supper approached, Big Tony and Albert were still asleep so Mrs Mouse gently woke them.

"Oh, I must have dropped off for a moment," said the little mouse, rubbing his eyes.

"A moment? You've both been asleep for nearly two hours," said his mother.

"Have I?" said Albert. "I'm not sure I'm cut out for this working business."

"Well, you've just got tomorrow and then Mr Wells will be back," said Mrs Mouse. "Anyway, supper is nearly ready."

Albert and Big Tony made their way into the kitchen and sat down at the table.

"So, Albert, did you do anything exciting today while you were Mayor?" asked Millie.

"Yes, I met lots of amazing people," said her brother.

"Well, come on, tell us all about your day," said his mother as she put the food on the plates.

"Ok, first, I visited every house on Victoria Road and introduced myself."

"What every house?" asked Millie. "Why?"

"I thought it would be good to meet the people of Dartmouth and just say hello. I asked them if they needed anything but most of them said they were fine."

Albert paused to eat some of his cheese pie.

"Then I had to visit the Memory Cafe. That's a place for people who feel lonely and want to meet other people. They talk about what life was like when they were young and sometimes they listen to music. Do you know that some of those people are older than me?"

"Please tell me that you had lunch?" asked his mother.

"I had the best lunch ever," said Albert. "While I was visiting houses on Victoria Road I met a group of people called the Dartmouth Litteracy Society and they help to keep Dartmouth clean. Mum, you won't believe how much rubbish there is just thrown in the hedges. "

"Lunch, Albert, what did you have for lunch?" asked his mother, worrying that he hadn't eaten anything.

"I'm getting to that part. Well, these people do this work for free, so I decided as Mayor I would say thank you to them by buying them lunch. I know that everyone likes fish and chips so I went to the wheelhouse. The manager there said I didn't have to pay, which was lucky because I think it would have been quite expensive."

"How many people were there?" asked Dorothy.

"Twelve, I think," said Albert counting his fingers. "Yes, twelve. Anyway, Geoff, he's my driver, dropped me off where the people were working and we all had fish and chips together. After that, I helped them pick up litter for the rest of the afternoon."

"No wonder you're tired, Albert," said his mother.

"So, what are you doing tomorrow?" asked Dorothy.

"I'm not sure. I need to check my diary when I get to the office," said Albert.

After supper, Big Tony went home and Albert said goodnight to his mother.

"Sleep well," said Mrs Mouse.

"I will," yawned Albert as he went upstairs to bed.

Chapter 27

Albert's alarm clock went off and the little mouse opened his eyes.

"What? It can't be morning already," he said throwing back his duvet.

Albert staggered to the bathroom and then got dressed. He was so tired that all he wanted to do was go back to sleep.

"Albert, your breakfast's ready," shouted his mother from downstairs.

"Just coming," said the little mouse as he picked up his cap.

"Do you feel better after a good night's sleep?" asked Mrs Mouse as Albert came into the kitchen.

"No, not really," said Albert yawning. "I really don't know how adults manage to work every day."

"We just get used to it, I suppose. Now hurry up, because the car will be here soon," said his mother.

Albert quickly ate his cereal and then put his bowl in the sink.

"Right, Mum, I'm off," he said hugging his mother.

The little mouse then opened the front door and walked down to the gate.

"Morning, Geoff," he said as he got in the car.

"Morning, Albert. Where is Big Tony?"

"Not sure, but if he's as tired as me he will probably still be asleep," sighed Albert. "He can catch up later."

Several minutes later, Geoff arrived outside the council offices and Albert hopped out of the car.

"Thanks, Geoff," he said and climbed up the steps.

"Good morning, Mayor," said Melanie. "I've made you a hot chocolate, it's on your desk."

"Thank you very much," said Albert as he went into his office.

The little mouse had just sat down at his desk and was checking his diary when the telephone rang.

"Hello, the Mayor of Dartmouth. How can I help you?" said Albert holding the phone to his ear.

"Morning, Albert, it's David. How are you?"

"I'm good. A bit tired if I'm honest. Yesterday was quite a busy day," said Albert.

"So I hear. The Memory Cafe said the visit went well so congratulations on that."

"Thanks, I really enjoyed meeting everyone," said the little mouse.

"Well, I have some good news. The doctors say if I'm careful I can come back to work tomorrow," said Mr Wells.

"That's great news," said Albert. "But can I ask you a question?"

"Of course."

"I've looked at my appointment for today and it says I am opening a Pet Tank?" said Albert.

"Ah, yes. It confused me for a moment. It's actually Pétanque which is a French game very much like bowling. Don't worry, there are no animals that might see you as lunch."

"Phew," said Albert, feeling a lot happier.

"Ok, well, I'll leave you to get on with the job. Thanks again Albert for helping like this," said Mr Wells.

"It's my pleasure, David. Goodbye!" said Albert, putting the phone down.

Chapter 28

After Albert had finished his hot chocolate, he spent the rest of the morning signing official council papers and letters. Albert enjoyed signing his name because it reminded him of the letter he'd written to Father Christmas.

Soon it was time for Albert to go and open the Pétanque Courts in Coronation Park. He put the signed letters in the wooden tray on his desk that had the word 'OUT' on it and then left his office.

The little mouse went downstairs where Geoff was waiting.

"All ready?" he asked opening the car door for Albert.

"Ready!" said Albert, putting on his seatbelt.

It only took a few minutes to reach Coronation Park where a large crowd had gathered. They all cheered as Albert got out of the car.

"Thank you, everyone. I'm so glad you have all come out to see the opening of these two Pétanque Courts. To be honest, I was a little nervous about this visit as I thought Pétanque was actually a Pet Tank and there might be snakes or something," said Albert smiling. "But I've found out that Pétanque is a French word. Anyway, it gives me great pleasure as Mayor of Dartmouth to officially open these courts."

As Albert held the purple ribbon he realised that he had forgotten to bring any scissors to cut the official opening ribbon.

"Here, let me help you," said Big Tony as he stepped out from the crowd and bit through the ribbon with his beak.

"Ladies and gentlemen, please give a big round of applause to my friend, Big Tony," said Albert.

Everyone cheered and clapped.

"Where were you this morning?" whispered Albert.

"Oh yes, sorry, I overslept," said the gull.

Albert turned to the crowd and held up his hands to call for quiet.

"Erm, I'd just like to say a few more words if I can. As many of you know I became your Mayor at very short notice due to Mr Wells breaking his leg. Being the Mayor of Dartmouth, even for these few days, has been one of the greatest pleasures of my life and one that I will always remember. I hope I have served you well as Mayor and I'd like to thank you all for the kindness and support you've shown me. Thank you."

"Three cheers for Albert! Hip hip hooray, hooray, hooray!" shouted the crowd.

Chapter 29

Several days later while Albert was still resting at home, there was a knock at the door.

Albert jumped down from the sofa and went to see who it was.

"Hello, Albert, how are you?" asked Mr Wells.

"Good morning, Mayor, what a nice surprise. Please, come in," said Albert.

"Thank you, but I can't stop. I just wanted to thank you on behalf of the town of Dartmouth for everything you did while you were Mayor," said David Wells.

The Mayor paused.

"Your kindness and thoughtfulness have been an inspiration to the people of Dartmouth," he said.

"It was nothing. I was just honoured that you asked me," said the little mouse.

"Well, I appreciate it," said Mr Wells, as he shook Albert's hand. "So, thank you very much."

"Oh, I almost forgot. Stay there," said Albert and he rushed upstairs to his bedroom.

He reached under his pillow and picked up the badge and then ran back downstairs.

"I forgot to give this back," said Albert, holding out the gold badge.

"You keep that, Albert," said the Mayor.

"Really!?" said the little mouse, hardly able to believe his ears.

"You deserve it. You've been a credit to this town. Anyway, I'd better get back, you know how it is? Busy, busy, busy," smiled the Mayor.

"I do," said Albert.

That evening, Albert sat on the sofa next to his mother admiring his golden badge.

"Did the Mayor really give you that to keep?" asked Millie.

"He certainly did. He said I was a credit to Dartmouth," said Albert.

"One day, I'd like to be a Mayor so I could get a badge like that too," said Millie.

"You don't become Mayor so you can get things," said Albert. "You become Mayor so you can give and do things for others."

"Like what?" his sister asked.

"Like being kind, helpful and thoughtful. There are a lot of people who don't have very much and it's important we try to help them. Then there are others, like the litter pickers, who gather up rubbish and don't ask for any money. Being Mayor has taught me that sometimes it's better to give than to receive. If we all did that, Dartmouth would be an even better place to live."

"Not only Dartmouth," said Mrs Mouse. "The whole world would be better if we were all kinder."

Albert nodded his head.

"I agree," he said, putting the badge back in his pocket, and smiling.

Did you enjoy reading about my adventures with my friend Big Tony?
I hope this story showed you that you can become anything you want, even the Mayor!
If you are in Dartmouth, please come and visit my house.
I will probably be in my bedroom window planning my next adventure.

Albert

The Albert Mouse Trail

Now you can visit the places that appear in the
Albert Mouse books.

Just look for these blue stickers around
Dartmouth.

*By Appointment to
children's imagination*

Be the first to know when James Hywel's next book is available!

Follow him at https://www.bookbub.com/author/james-hywel to get an alert whenever he has a new release, preorder, or discount!

You can also sign up for our blog at
https://jameshywel.com/blog
Thank you, he appreciates your support!

Acknowledgements

I'm grateful to Brian and Pam, the human owners of Cherub Cottage, for sharing their house with Albert and his family.

I'm especially grateful to **The Mayor of Dartmouth, Cllr David Wells**, for being the driving force behind this story and for allowing Albert to be Mayor for the day.
I'd also like to thank the **Town Councillors** for allowing us to use the Dartmouth Town Council emblem on this book's cover.

Thanks also to **Dartmouth Caring** and the **Memory Cafe**. Especially to Nick Hindmarsh, Kay Pratley, Buffy Matheson, Natasha Branton, Sarah Dorsett, Ellie, Gill, Beryl and Tom.

I'd also like to that the **Dartmouth Litteracy Society** for the hours they spend gathering up discarded rubbish. Especially Andora, Sophie, Elaine, Isla, Finley, Sarah, Oli, Andy, Chris, Ruth, Hazel and Sam.

Thank you to the people of Dartmouth for welcoming me into their vibrant town with abundant charm and seafaring history.

Thanks to my 'BETA Readers' - Kate, Sarah, Andrea, Jude and John.

As always I am grateful to "Walter" for sending me the breeze that moves the willows.

About James Hywel

James Hywel is a children's author and creator
of both Mr Milliner and Albert Mouse.
He is a member of *The Royal Society of Literature,
The Society of Authors, The Writers Guild of Great
Britain* and *The Dartmouth & Kingswear Society*.

For more books and updates visit our website:
www.jameshywel.com

Remember to sign up for our blog
https://jameshywel.com/blog

Break The Cycle C.I.C helps children and young people benefit from bespoke educational programmes that support their development, helping them to navigate their thoughts and feelings, and appreciate their time in and out of school. Thus, supporting positive relationships and challenging negative behaviour.

Albert is excited to be visiting schools with his friend Sarah to talk to children who are feeling anxious, nervous, upset, worried or confused. Albert feels many of the same feelings as other children his age do.

www.jameshywel.com/break-the-cycle

Break The Cycle C.I.C.

Company Number 14265959

Printed in Great Britain
by Amazon